AP® English Literature Skills Practice Workbook

to accompany

Ideas in Literature

Building Skills and Understanding

for the AP® English Literature Course

John R. Williamson Mary Jo Zell Elizabeth Davis

bedford, freeman & worth publishers
Boston | New York

ISBN-13: 978-1-319-51787-8

Printed in the United States of America
2 3 4 5 6 28 27 26 25 24

Bedford, Freeman & Worth Publishers
120 Broadway, Floor 25
New York, NY 10271
https://www.bfwpub.com/high-school/us

Table of Contents

UNIT 1

Reading Literally and Figuratively

Ideas in Literature, **1e**
Unit 1, p. 12

As you read Stephen King's "Here There Be Tygers," think about how the details of the story contribute to your understanding of the main character. Use the following graphic organizer to capture details from the text and describe what they reveal about Charles.

Analyzing Character	
Speech • What does a character say? • How does a character speak?	
Details from the text:	What does this reveal about the character?
Action • What choices does a character make? • How does the character interact with others? • Is the character's behavior consistent? • What does a character do when alone?	
Details from the text:	What does this reveal about the character?
Description • What physical features does the character have? • What is the character wearing? • What might a character's background reveal about him or her? • What words and phrases do the narrator or other characters use to describe the character? • What might the character's name reveal about their personality?	
Details from the text:	What does this reveal about the character?

***Ideas in Literature*, 1e**

Unit 1, p. 21

As you read "Another April," record details from the story that describe place, time, or the physical environment. Then consider what those details reveal about the values of the setting.

<table>
<tr><th colspan="2">Analyzing Setting</th></tr>
<tr><td colspan="2">Place
• Is the location urban or rural?
• Is the location nondescript? Could it take place anywhere in the world?
• Is the story set in a significant cultural or religious location?
• Is the setting physically isolated or deeply integrated into a community?
• Does the story take place inside or outside?</td></tr>
<tr><td>Details from the text:</td><td>What does this reveal about the setting?</td></tr>
<tr><td colspan="2">Time
• Does the story take place in the past, present, or future?
• Is the story happening in a particular historical period?
• What season of the year is it?
• What day, week, or month is it?
• What time of day does the story take place or span?
• Are the characters recognizing any holidays or events?
• How long does the story take place? Minutes? Hours? A day? Multiple days? A year? Multiple years?</td></tr>
<tr><td>Details from the text:</td><td>What does this reveal about the setting?</td></tr>
</table>

Physical Environment • What geographical location is the setting for the story? Do you know the country/territory, state, city, town, neighborhood, or location? • How is the landscape described? • What are the weather conditions and climate like? • Are there natural features (such as the forest, the sea, or the mountains)? • Are there constructed features (such as a hospital, an ice skating rink, or a bridge)?	
Details from the text:	What does this reveal about the setting?

***Ideas in Literature*, 1e**
Unit 1, p. 38

Identify the details of the text that describe each part of the plot in "The Parable of the Prodigal Son." Then create an illustration of the story's plot that depicts the relationship between each event and shows how these events create the story's narrative arc.

Analyzing Plot		
Considerations: • In what ways does the story's plot develop a narrative arc? • How does a story's plot develop a dramatic situation? • What character relationships are revealed through the story's plot? • How does the conflict reflect a tension of values? • How does the story's resolution reveal an interpretation?		
Beginning • Exposition • Narrative hook	**Middle** • Rising action • Climax	**End** • Falling action • Resolution
Plot details:	Plot details:	Plot details:
Illustration of the narrative arc of the plot:		

***Ideas in Literature*, 1e**
Unit 1, p. 45

Identify the type of point of view in “Sweetness.” Provide details from the story that reveal that point of view. Finally, explain the effect that this type of point of view has on the story as a whole.

Analyzing Narration	
Point of view:	
Details from the Story That Reveal Point of View	**Effect on the Narrative**

***Ideas in Literature*, 1e**
Unit 1, p. 94

Review the details from the text you are analyzing for your literary argument. Record details for each of the text elements in the column. Next, consider how these details reveal a unifying idea and an insight. Record these in the right column.

Determining a Unifying Idea and Insight	
Idea:	
Story Elements	**Details**
Characters	
Setting	
Structure	
Narration	
Idea + insight:	

***Ideas in Literature*, 1e**
Unit 1, p. 95

In the following chart, record the title, author, and focus in the left column and then add your unifying idea and insight about that idea. Putting these pieces together will result in a workable thesis statement.

Developing a Thesis Statement		
Topic	**Claim**	
Title, Author, and Focus (author choices)	**Unifying Idea** **+**	**Insight**

***Ideas in Literature*, 1e**
Unit 1, p. 96

Review your text for a unifying idea and literary elements (character, setting, plot structure, and narration). Next, complete the graphic organizer to plan your thesis statement and focus for each body paragraph.

Organizing a Literary Argument		
Defensible Thesis Statement with Claim (idea + insight):		
Topic Sentence 1 (Focus of paragraph related to unifying idea):	**Topic Sentence 2** (Focus of paragraph related to unifying idea):	**Topic Sentence 3** (Focus of paragraph related to unifying idea):

***Ideas in Literature*, 1e**
Unit 1, p. 99

Write your thesis statement and then draft two or more body paragraphs to support your claim (idea + insight). Your body paragraphs should begin with topic sentences that include a focus for the paragraph related to your unifying idea. Next, include evidence from the text to support the focus in the paragraph. Finally, write a concluding statement that expresses the relevance of the unifying idea.

<table>
<tr><th colspan="3">Incorporating Supporting Evidence</th></tr>
<tr><td colspan="3">Defensible Thesis Statement with Claim (idea + insight):</td></tr>
<tr><td colspan="3"></td></tr>
<tr><td>Topic Sentence 1
(Focus of the paragraph related to the unifying idea):</td><td>Topic Sentence 2
(Focus of the paragraph related to the unifying idea):</td><td>Topic Sentence 3
(Focus of the paragraph related to the unifying idea):</td></tr>
<tr><td></td><td></td><td></td></tr>
<tr><td>Evidence:</td><td>Evidence:</td><td>Evidence:</td></tr>
<tr><td></td><td></td><td></td></tr>
<tr><td colspan="3">Conclusion (Relevance of idea):</td></tr>
<tr><td colspan="3"></td></tr>
</table>

***Ideas in Literature*, 1e**
Unit 1, p. 100

After you have completed revising and editing your own argument, review another student's literary argument and provide helpful feedback.

Revising and Editing a Literary Argument		
Revising and Editing Checklist	**Unit 1 Focus Skills**	**Comment on the Effectiveness and/or Make a Suggestion**
Does the thesis statement convey an interpretation? Does the interpretation include an idea and an insight?	Defensible thesis	
Does the writer provide a focus for each body paragraph to develop the idea and insight in the thesis? Is the unifying idea reflected in each topic sentence?	Topic sentences	
Does the writer provide evidence to support the interpretation in the thesis?	Supporting evidence	
Does the writer demonstrate control over the conventions of writing?	Conventions	

UNIT 2

Analyzing Comparisons and Representations

***Ideas in Literature*, 1e**
Unit 2, p. 122

As you read "Verses upon the Burning of our House," consider how details in the poem help reveal the speaker's perspective. Record your notes in the graphic organizer.

Describing a Character's Perspective		
Considerations	**Details from the Text**	**What the Details Reveal about Perspective**
Character's background		
Character's actions and choices		
Character's internal thoughts		
Dialogue		
Interactions with others		

***Ideas in Literature*, 1e**
Unit 2, p. 130

Read the following poem, "Janet Waking." As you read, consider whether the author incorporates a primary shift or a series of contrasts in the text. Then, record details from the poem in the following graphic organizer, which will help you make an interpretation.

<table>
<tr><th colspan="2">Analyzing Shifts and Contrasts</th></tr>
<tr><td colspan="2">Indicators of Shifts
• Contrasting transition words (e.g., but, however, yet)
• Syntactic markers (e.g., isolated simple sentences)
• Punctuation (e.g., use of question mark, dash, colon, parentheses)
• Structural changes (e.g., change in paragraph or stanza, one-sentence paragraphs)
• A change in the connotation of words or language

Indicators of Contrasts
• A back-and-forth movement in dialogue, plot, or other elements that create contrast
• Frequent changes in speaker, imagery, point of view
• Juxtaposed characters, settings, points of view, or images (e.g., I and we; then and now)</td></tr>
<tr><td>Shift (detail before) or
Contrast (details of Side A)</td><td>Shift (after) or
Contrasts (details Side B)</td></tr>
<tr><td>Indication in the text:</td><td>Indication in the text:</td></tr>
<tr><td colspan="2">What is revealed through these contrasts or shifts?</td></tr>
</table>

***Ideas in Literature*, 1e**
Unit 2, p. 137

As you read White's poem, look for examples of repetition and referents that emphasize her message. Record those examples and explain how they contribute to her message.

Explaining the Function of Words and Phrases		
Literary Element	**Examples from the Text**	**Effect**
Antecedents: Authors refer to nouns, pronouns, phrases, or clauses expressed in earlier parts of a text. The first or initial instance is called the antecedent of the referent.		
Repetition: Repetition occurs when a writer uses the exact word or phrase consecutively or throughout a text.		
Alliteration is a type of repetition when consonant sounds at the beginning of multiple consecutive or closely placed words in a text.		

***Ideas in Literature*, 1e**
Unit 2, p. 144

As you read the following poem by e.e. cummings, use the graphic organizer to record details from the poem of the comparison in the poem. Explain the significance of each aspect of the traits being compared.

Explaining the Function of Comparisons		
Considerations • Which two objects are being compared in a particular metaphor? • What are the particular traits and characteristics being compared? • What is significant about the selection of the objects being compared? • How does a comparison through a metaphor contribute to meaning in the text? • How might the figurative meaning of a metaphor depend on the context in which it is presented? • How does a metaphorical comparison contribute to the figurative meaning of a character, conflict, setting, theme, etc.?		
Metaphorical Object	**Idea of Human Experience**	**Significance of Comparison**

Ideas in Literature, 1e
Unit 2, p. 183

Review the text that you are analyzing for your literary argument. Identify the unifying idea that will guide your analysis. Record this in the first row. Then, in the left column, record details related to that idea for each of the figurative elements that you have identified. In the right column, record how these details lead you to an insight about that idea. Next, consider the associations that you have made from your reading to determine the tone (or different tones) in the text.

Analyzing Tone through Figurative Elements	
Idea:	
Textual Details	**Insights and Connections to Unifying Idea**
Tone(s):	
Idea + insight:	

***Ideas in Literature*, 1e**
Unit 2, p. 185

Record the unifying idea and insight of the text you are analyzing in the following graphic organizer. Next, using the thesis templates as a guide, write a defensible thesis statement. You may choose whether or not to preview your line of reasoning.

Developing a Thesis Statement for Tone Analysis		
Topic	**Claim**	
Title, Author, and Focus (author choices)	**Unifying Idea** **+**	**Insight**

***Ideas in Literature*, 1e**
Unit 2, p. 188

Review your thesis statement, which may or may not preview the line of reasoning. Record the topic sentences to represent your line of reasoning and place them in a logical order. As you do this, consider the potential evidence from the text that helped you arrive at your line of reasoning. That textual evidence will serve as support for each of your techniques.

Developing a Line of Reasoning		
Defensible Thesis Statement with Interpretation (idea + insight):		
Topic Sentence 1 (Author's first technique that contributes to tone and illustrates unifying idea):	**Topic Sentence 2** (Author's second technique that contributes to tone and illustrates unifying idea):	**Topic Sentence 3** (Author's third technique that contributes to tone and illustrates unifying idea):

***Ideas in Literature*, 1e**
Unit 2, p. 189

Write your thesis statement and develop a logical line of reasoning to support your interpretation. Next, draft two or more body paragraphs that include textual evidence from the text to support each reason. Finally, write a concluding statement that explains the significance of your idea. You may use the following table for planning.

Selecting Relevant Evidence to Support a Line of Reasoning		
Defensible Thesis Statement with Interpretation (idea + insight):		
Topic Sentence 1 (Identify the author's first technique that contributes to tone and illustrates unifying idea):	**Topic Sentence 2** (Identify the author's second technique that contributes to tone and illustrates unifying idea):	**Topic Sentence 3** (Identify the author's third technique that contributes to tone and illustrates unifying idea):
Relevant Evidence:	**Relevant Evidence:**	**Relevant Evidence:**

Commentary (Link the evidence to your thesis by explaining its significance in relation to the claim in your thesis):	**Commentary** (Link the evidence to your thesis by explaining its significance in relation to the claim in your thesis):	**Commentary** (Link the evidence to your thesis by explaining its significance in relation to the claim in your thesis):

Note: Your argument should include the number of reasons necessary to justify your claim. These organizers are illustrative of three reasons. Your argument may include more or fewer.

***Ideas in Literature*, 1e**
Unit 2, p. 191

When you have completed your final body paragraph, add a sentence or two at the end of your argument in which you explain the relevance of the unifying idea in your thesis.

Explaining the Relevance of the Idea
Unifying idea:
Relevance of the idea:

Ideas in Literature, 1e
Unit 2, p. 192

After you have completed revising and editing your own argument, review another student's literary argument and provide helpful feedback.

Revising and Editing an Analysis of Tone		
Revising and Editing Checklist	**Unit 2 Focus Skills**	**Comment on the Effectiveness and/or Make a Suggestion**
Does the thesis statement identify one or more tones and convey an interpretation? Does the interpretation connect to a unifying idea and an insight?	Defensible thesis	
Does the writer provide a logical line of reasoning to develop the idea and insight in the thesis? Is the unifying idea evident in this line of reasoning?	Line of reasoning	
Does the writer provide evidence for each topic sentence to support the interpretation in the thesis? Does the evidence defend the choice of tone(s) identified in the thesis?	Relevant evidence	

Does the concluding statement explain the significance of the unifying idea?	Contextualizing the argument	
Does the writer demonstrate control over the conventions of writing?	Conventions	

UNIT 3

Analyzing Tensions

As you read *Mistaken Identity*, identify physical, social, behavioral, emotional, psychological, and spiritual details that establish each character. Consider whether either of the characters changes in any of these aspects. If so, note the details after the shift. Then, explain the significance of that change in relation to the play's conflict.

Analyzing Dynamic Characters			
	Textual Details before the Shift	**Textual Details after the Change**	**Significance**
Physical			
Social			
Behavioral			
Emotional			
Psychological			
Spiritual			

***Ideas in Literature*, 1e**
Unit 3, p. 220

As you read the play *Los Vendidos*, identify details of the story that reveal aspects of the social, cultural, and historical context. Consider how each of these details may contribute to your interpretation of the story.

Analyzing Setting and Context		
Context	**Aspects**	**Details from the Story and Significance**
Social	• Event • Occasion • Class • Living and working conditions	
Cultural	• Religion, beliefs, and shared stories • Traditions and customs • Manners • Identity	
Historical	• Historical events • Innovations, discoveries • Conventions • Diction: historical meaning of words	

***Ideas in Literature*, 1e**
Unit 3, p. 231

As you read *Naked Lunch*, identify the important moments of the play. What do the characters' actions and decisions reveal about them? Explain how each of these moments contributes to the central conflict. Which moment in the sequence could be identified as the climax? How is the conflict resolved?

Analyzing Conflict		
Moment: Problem and Type of Conflict	**Action/Decision:** Character Action or Decisions	**Importance:** Effect on Next or Other Events of the Plot, Especially the Primary Conflict or Story's Resolution

***Ideas in Literature*, 1e**
Unit 3, p. 386

Review the text that you are analyzing for your literary argument. Record your unifying idea, as well as the topic and focus of your analysis. Then, use the graphic organizer to identify details and their significance for different moments in the work. (You may need to delete or add rows.)

Analyzing a Character		
Unifying idea:		
Topic and focus of analysis:		
Section of the Text	**Details from the Text**	**Insights and Connections to the Unifying Idea**

Ideas in Literature, 1e
Unit 3, p. 388

Record the unifying idea and insight of the text you are analyzing in the following graphic organizer. Next, using the thesis templates as a guide, write a defensible thesis statement. You may choose whether or not to preview your line of reasoning.

Developing a Thesis Statement for Character Analysis		
Topic	**Claim**	
Title, Author, and Focus (aspect of character)	**Unifying Idea** **+**	**Insight**

***Ideas in Literature*, 1e**
Unit 3, p. 390

Review your thesis statement, which may or may not preview the line of reasoning. Record the topic sentences to represent your line of reasoning and place them in a logical order. As you do this, consider the potential evidence from the text that helped you arrive at your line of reasoning. That textual evidence will serve as support for these reasons.

<table>
<tr><th colspan="3">Developing a Line of Reasoning</th></tr>
<tr><td colspan="3">Defensible Thesis Statement with Claim (idea + insight):</td></tr>
<tr><td colspan="3"></td></tr>
<tr><td>Topic Sentence 1
(Identify the first aspect of the character related to the unifying idea):</td><td>Topic Sentence 2
(Identify the second aspect of the character related to the unifying idea):</td><td>Topic Sentence 3
(Identify the third aspect of the character related to the unifying idea):</td></tr>
<tr><td></td><td></td><td></td></tr>
</table>

Ideas in Literature, 1e
Unit 3, p. 392

Write your thesis statement and develop a logical line of reasoning to support your interpretation. Carefully organize your body paragraphs and arrange the evidence within them. Next, draft two or more body paragraphs that include evidence from the text to support each reason. Include transitions to link your reasons and evidence to your claim.

Incorporating Relevant and Sufficient Evidence		
Defensible Thesis Statement with Claim (idea + insight):		
Topic Sentence 1 (Identify the first aspect of the character related to the unifying idea):	**Topic Sentence 2** (Identify the second aspect of the character related to the unifying idea):	**Topic Sentence 3** (Identify the third aspect of the character related to the unifying idea):
Textual Details (Relevant and sufficient evidence):	**Textual Details** (Relevant and sufficient evidence):	**Textual Details** (Relevant and sufficient evidence):

***Ideas in Literature*, 1e**
Unit 3, p. 395

Build on your emerging literary argument by adding commentary to your relevant and sufficient evidence. As you plan your explanation, carefully consider your unifying idea so that you may carry this idea throughout your argument in a unified way.

Linking Evidence to the Line of Reasoning		
Defensible Thesis Statement with Claim (idea + insight):		
Topic Sentence 1 (Identify the first aspect of the character related to the unifying idea):	**Topic Sentence 2** (Identify the second aspect of the character related to the unifying idea):	**Topic Sentence 3** (Identify the third aspect of the character related to the unifying idea):
Textual Details (Relevant and sufficient evidence):	**Textual Details** (Relevant and sufficient evidence):	**Textual Details** (Relevant and sufficient evidence):
Signal phrase and evidence 1: Signal phrase and evidence 2:	Signal phrase and evidence 1: Signal phrase and evidence 2:	Signal phrase and evidence 1: Signal phrase and evidence 2:

Commentary (Link evidence to reason and idea):	**Commentary** (Link evidence to reason and idea):	**Commentary** (Link evidence to reason and idea):
Sentence stem and explanation of function of evidence:	Sentence stem and explanation of function of evidence:	Sentence stem and explanation of function of evidence:

***Ideas in Literature*, 1e**
Unit 3, p. 396

In the chart below, record some notes to help you communicate the context of your argument, along with other introductory material that will funnel your ideas to your thesis statement. Next, record ideas to help you explain the relevance of your idea and insight in your concluding statements.

Introducing Your Literary Argument	
Introducing Context	
Title, Author, Genre	
Character and Narrative Situation	
Thesis	

***Ideas in Literature*, 1e**
Unit 3, p. 397

After you have completed revising and editing your own argument, review another student's literary argument and provide helpful feedback.

Revising and Editing a Character Analysis		
Revising and Editing Checklist	**Unit 3 Focus Skills**	**Comment on the Effectiveness and/or Make a Suggestion**
Does the writer include the narrative situation and perspective, title, and author of the literary text in the first paragraph? Does the brief summary of context lead to the idea?	Introductions for character analysis	
Does the thesis statement convey an interpretation? Does the interpretation connect to an idea and an insight?	Defensible thesis	
Does the writer provide a logical sequence of reasons to support the idea and insight in the thesis? Are these reasons linked to the claim with transitions?	Line of reasoning: Unity	

Does the writer provide relevant and sufficient evidence to support the interpretation in the thesis? Is the evidence linked to the topic sentences with transitions?	Relevant and sufficient evidence: Coherence	
Does the writer explain how the evidence supports a reason and connects to the interpretation in the thesis? Does the commentary connect to the unifying idea?	Commentary: Unity	
Does the writer explain the argument's significance within a broader context?	Relevance	
Does the writer demonstrate control over the conventions of writing?	Conventions	

UNIT 4
Analyzing Perspectives

***Ideas in Literature*, 1e**
Unit 4, p. 424

As you read "A Good Man Is Hard to Find," record details about the characters and conflict. Identify the protagonist's choices, as well as the values represented by the protagonist and antagonist. Use these details as you analyze the story's resolution.

Analyzing Characters in Conflict		
	Protagonist:	**Antagonist:**
Type of Conflict		
Description of Characters		
Choices Made by Protagonist		
Values Represented by Character		

***Ideas in Literature*, 1e**
Unit 4, p. 445

Describe the physical, social, cultural, and historical setting of "A Rose for Emily." Note the details from the story that convey the different types of settings. Analyze how the details of setting contribute to your interpretation of the text.

Analyzing the Significance of Setting		
Types of Setting	**Key Questions**	**Details from the Story and Significance**
Physical Setting (the place where the story is set)	• What is the location? And what values are embodied in that location? • Why might the time of day or time of year be important? • What might the weather reveal? • How is nature portrayed or presented? • How might aspects of the physical environment or nature reflect aspects of a character?	
Social Setting (how people live and what they believe at the time the story is set)	• What do the descriptions, the physical objects, and possessions reveal? • Are there works of art present? If so, why? • Does the setting encompass a social event (e.g., wedding, funeral, festival)? Why might this be important? • What role does religion or faith play?	

Cultural Setting (the arts and popular interests of the time the story is set)	• How does the urban or rural setting affect the characters? • What might the description of buildings or other structures and their proximity to each other reveal?	
Historical Setting (the events in history that occurred at the time the story is set)	• How does when the story is set affect the reader's understanding? • What values are associated with the historical setting? • How do a character's actions and values fit within the historical setting?	

***Ideas in Literature*, 1e**
Unit 4, p. 465

As you read "Red," record details about the characters and the conflict. Reflect on the choices that the protagonist makes and the values represented by both the protagonist and antagonist. Use these details as you analyze how the story's resolution contributes to your interpretation of the text.

Analyzing Archetypes		
Type	**Examples from the Story**	**Significance**
Situational archetypes: • Battle • Coming of age • Fall • Initiation • Intervention • Journey • Quest • Redemption • Supernatural		
Character archetypes: • Caregiver • Christ figure • Confidante • Devil figure • Earth mother • Fool • Friendly beast • Hero • Innocent • Outcast/outsider • Rebel • Scapegoat • Soothsayer/sage • Star-crossed lovers • Temptress • Wolf in sheep's clothing		

Symbol archetypes: • Blindness • Colors • Communion • Day cycles • Disease • Food • Illness • Light and dark • Magic weapon • Rain • Seasons • Water		
Setting archetypes: • City/urban area • Desert • Forest/wilderness • Garden/paradise • Island • River • Rural areas • Sea • Space • Underworld • Unfamiliar places • Utopia • West		

***Ideas in Literature*, 1e**
Unit 4, p. 477

As you read "Interpreter of Maladies," consider the narrative perspective and distance of the narrator. How does Lahiri's use of these techniques contribute to her tone and your interpretation of the story?

Connecting Narration and Tone		
	Details from the Text	**What the Details Reveal about Tone**
Narrative Perspective		
Narrative Distance		
Narrator's Tone		

***Ideas in Literature*, 1e**
Unit 4, p. 536

Consider the text that you are analyzing and complete the following table. In the middle column, record specific details from the text related to the narrator of the story. In the right- and column, explain the effect of the author's choice of narrator and narrative distance on the perspective. Be sure to connect these details to your unifying idea.

Analyzing a Narrator's Perspective		
Unifying idea:		
Topic and focus of analysis:		
Narrator	**Details from the Text**	**Implications for Narrative Perspective**
First or third person		
Background, values, experiences		
Distance from events		
Distance in time		
Narrator's tone or attitude		

***Ideas in Literature*, 1e**
Unit 4, p. 537

In the first column record the title, author, and aspect of focus as your topic. Use the remaining columns to record the unifying idea and insight of the text you are analyzing. You may choose whether or not to preview your line of reasoning.

Developing a Thesis Statement for Analysis of Perspective		
Topic	**Claim**	
Title, Author, and Focus (aspect of perspective)	**Unifying Idea +**	**Insight**

***Ideas in Literature*, 1e**
Unit 4, p. 539

Review the idea and insight in your thesis statement and choose a logical line of reasoning to support your thesis. Compose two or more supporting topic sentences and organize them in a logical sequence that represents your train of thought. Highlight the words related to your unifying idea and underline words that link one topic sentence to another.

Achieving Unity through a Line of Reasoning		
Defensible Thesis Statement with Claim (idea + insight):		
Topic Sentence 1 (Identify the first aspect of the perspective related to the unifying idea):	**Topic Sentence 2** (Identify the second aspect of the perspective related to the unifying idea):	**Topic Sentence 3** (Identify the third aspect of the perspective related to the unifying idea):

***Ideas in Literature*, 1e**
Unit 4, p. 540

Write your thesis statement (idea + insight) and develop a logical line of reasoning to support your interpretation. Then carefully organize your body paragraphs and arrange the evidence within them. Next, draft two or more body paragraphs that include evidence from the text to support each reason. Include transitions to link your reasons and evidence to your claim.

Arranging Evidence for Unity and Coherence		
Defensible Thesis Statement with Claim (idea + insight):		
Topic Sentence 1 (Identify the first aspect of the perspective related to the unifying idea):	**Topic Sentence 2** (Identify the second aspect of the perspective related to the unifying idea):	**Topic Sentence 3** (Identify the third aspect of the perspective related to the unifying idea):
Textual Details (Relevant and sufficient evidence):	**Textual Details** (Relevant and sufficient evidence):	**Textual Details** (Relevant and sufficient evidence):

***Ideas in Literature*, 1e**
Unit 4, p. 543

Continue developing your literary argument by planning and writing helpful commentary that links your evidence to both your line of reasoning and the idea in your claim. Consult the reference chart "Creating Unity through Commentary" for sentence stems to help you write your explanations.

<table>
<tr><th colspan="3">Creating Unity through Commentary</th></tr>
<tr><td colspan="3">Defensible Thesis Statement with Claim (idea + insight):</td></tr>
<tr><td colspan="3"></td></tr>
<tr><td>Topic Sentence 1
(Identify the first aspect of the perspective related to the unifying idea):</td><td>Topic Sentence 2
(Identify the second aspect of the perspective related to the unifying idea):</td><td>Topic Sentence 3
(Identify the third aspect of the perspective related to the unifying idea):</td></tr>
<tr><td></td><td></td><td></td></tr>
<tr><td>Textual Details
(Relevant and sufficient evidence):</td><td>Textual Details
(Relevant and sufficient evidence):</td><td>Textual Details
(Relevant and sufficient evidence):</td></tr>
<tr><td></td><td></td><td></td></tr>
</table>

Commentary (Link evidence to reason and idea):	**Commentary** (Link evidence to reason and idea):	**Commentary** (Link evidence to reason and idea):
Sentence stem and explanation of the function of evidence:	Sentence stem and explanation of the function of evidence:	Sentence stem and explanation of the function of evidence:

***Ideas in Literature*, 1e**
Unit 4, p. 544

In the following chart, record some notes to help you communicate the context of your argument, introductory details about the narrator, and introductory material that will funnel your ideas to your thesis statement. Next, record details to help you explain the relevance of your idea and insight in your concluding statements.

Establishing Context and Explaining Relevance	
Idea and Insight	**Context for Introduction**
	Significance of Idea in Conclusion

***Ideas in Literature*, 1e**
Unit 4, p. 545

After you have completed revising and editing your own argument, review another student's literary argument and provide helpful feedback.

Revising and Editing an Analysis of Perspective		
Revising and Editing Checklist	**Unit 4 Focus Skills**	**Comment on the Effectiveness and/or Make a Suggestion**
Does the writer include the author, title, narrative situation, and narrative perspective in the first paragraph? Does the brief summary of context lead to the idea?	Introductions for narrative perspective	
Does the thesis statement convey an interpretation? Does the interpretation connect to an idea and an insight?	Defensible thesis	
Does the writer provide a logical sequence of reasons to support the idea and insight in the thesis? Are these reasons linked to the claim with transitions?	Line of reasoning: Unity	

Does the writer provide relevant and sufficient evidence to support the interpretation in the thesis? Is the evidence linked to the topic sentences with transitions?	Relevant and sufficient evidence: Coherence	
Does the writer explain how the evidence supports a reason and connects to the interpretation in the thesis? Does the commentary connect to the unifying idea?	Commentary: Unity	
Does the writer explain the argument's significance within a broader context?	Relevance	
Does the writer demonstrate control over the conventions of writing?	Conventions	

UNIT 5

Analyzing Comparisons

***Ideas in Literature*, 1e**
Unit 5, p. 570

As you read Chan's poem, note how she draws upon the conventions of poetic forms, structures, and sound to convey her message.

Analyzing Structure and Sound in Poetry		
Author's Choices	**Key Considerations**	**Details and Effects**
Type: Narrative Lyric Epic Dramatic	How is the type of poetry related to the poet's purpose? How does the poem's context affect the poet's choice of type?	
Form and Structure: Closed Open	How does an author's choice of closed or open form contribute to a reader's interpretation? How does one part or section of a text relate to another part? How does one part or section of a text relate to the text as a whole? How does the structure of a poem contribute to a reader's interpretation?	
Sound: Rhythm Rhyme	How do rhyme and rhythm (e.g., rhyme scheme, meter, slant rhyme) contribute to the poem? How does the punctuation (or lack of punctuation) convey relationships and pauses that contribute to the interpretation of a poem?	

***Ideas in Literature*, 1e**
Unit 5, p. 577

As you read "The Lanyard," identify aspects of its imagery. Consider how the words and images affect the reader and contribute to an interpretation of the poem.

Analyzing Imagery		
Aspect of Imagery	**Details from the Poem**	**Effect on Reader**
Word Choice • Denotation • Connotation • Pun		
Images • Sensory Image • Imagery • Motif		
Exaggeration • Hyperbole • Understatement		

***Ideas in Literature*, 1e**
Unit 5, p. 586

As you read Heaney's poem, identify his use of figurative elements by noting particular textual details. Then, use the key considerations to explain the effect of the figurative elements.

Analyzing Comparisons		
Literary Element	**Key Considerations**	**Details from the Text and Effect**
Metaphor	What is being compared? Is this comparison extended throughout the text? What type of comparison is it? Why is this significant?	
Extended metaphor	What particular traits, qualities, or characteristics are being compared? Why did the author choose this particular metaphor? How is this metaphor relevant at the time the work was written? How is this metaphor relevant today?	

Allusion	Why did the author choose this particular reference? What does this allusion reveal about the author? What does this allusion reveal about the audience's relationship to the author? What are the points of comparison between the allusion (or its text of origin) and the text you're reading? How does this allusion fit into a larger motif? Does this text speak to another text? How? Why?	
Personification	What physical object or idea is being assigned human qualities? Which human qualities are being assigned? Why might this be important? Why did the author humanize this particular object or idea?	

***Ideas in Literature*, 1e**
Unit 5, p. 654

Consider the text you are analyzing and complete the following table. Choose a pattern of images or extended comparisons to explore in your analysis. In the middle column, record specific details of the images or comparisons from your text. In the right-hand column, explain the implications of the imagery or extended comparison. Be sure to connect these details to your unifying idea.

Analyzing Imagery and Extended Metaphor		
Unifying idea:		
Topic and focus of analysis:		
Literary Element	**Details from the Text**	**Insights and Connections to Unifying Idea**
Pattern of Images		
or		
Pattern of Comparisons		

***Ideas in Literature*, 1e**
Unit 5, p. 656

Complete the following chart. In the left column, record the title, author, and aspect of imagery or extended metaphor that you will explore. Next, record the unifying idea and insight that will convey your interpretation of your claim.

Developing a Thesis Statement for Analysis of Imagery/Extended Metaphor		
Topic	**Claim**	
Title, Author, and Focus (aspect of imagery or extended metaphor)	**Unifying Idea +**	**Insight**

Ideas in Literature, 1e
Unit 5, p. 658

Review the idea and insight in your thesis statement and then choose a logical line of reasoning to support your thesis. Compose two or more supporting topic sentences and organize them in a logical sequence that represents your train of thought. Highlight the words related to your unifying idea and underline words that link one topic sentence to another.

<table>
<tr><th colspan="3">Organizing an Analysis of Imagery/Extended Metaphor</th></tr>
<tr><td colspan="3">Defensible Thesis Statement with Claim (idea + insight):</td></tr>
<tr><td colspan="3"></td></tr>
<tr><td>Topic Sentence 1
(Identify the first aspect of imagery/extended metaphor related to the unifying idea):</td><td>Topic Sentence 2
(Identify the second aspect of imagery/extended metaphor related to the unifying idea):</td><td>Topic Sentence 3
(Identify the third aspect of imagery/extended metaphor related to the unifying idea):</td></tr>
<tr><td></td><td></td><td></td></tr>
</table>

***Ideas in Literature*, 1e**
Unit 5, p. 659

Write your thesis statement and develop a logical line of reasoning to support your interpretation. Carefully organize your body paragraphs and arrange the evidence within them. Next, draft two or more body paragraphs that include evidence from the text to support each reason. Include transitions to link your reasons and evidence to your claim.

Selecting and Arranging Relevant Evidence		
Defensible Thesis Statement with Claim (idea + insight):		
Topic Sentence 1 (First aspect of imagery/extended metaphor related to the unifying idea):	**Topic Sentence 2** (Second aspect of imagery/extended metaphor related to the unifying idea):	**Topic Sentence 3** (Third aspect of imagery/extended metaphor related to the unifying idea):
Textual Details (Relevant and sufficient evidence):	**Textual Details** (Relevant and sufficient evidence):	**Textual Details** (Relevant and sufficient evidence):

***Ideas in Literature*, 1e**
Unit 5, p. 662

Continue developing your literary argument by planning and writing helpful commentary that links your evidence to your line of reasoning and the idea in your claim. Continue practicing with the templates you used in Unit 4. In addition, incorporate transitions within and between paragraphs to create coherence.

Explaining the Relevance of Imagery/Extended Metaphor		
Defensible Thesis Statement with Claim (idea + insight):		
Topic Sentence 1 (First aspect of imagery/extended metaphor related to the unifying idea):	**Topic Sentence 2** (Second aspect of imagery/extended metaphor related to the unifying idea):	**Topic Sentence 3** (Third aspect of imagery/extended metaphor related to the unifying idea):
Textual Details (Relevant and sufficient evidence):	**Textual Details** (Relevant and sufficient evidence):	**Textual Details** (Relevant and sufficient evidence):

Commentary (Link evidence to reason and idea):	**Commentary** (Link evidence to reason and idea):	**Commentary** (Link evidence to reason and idea):
Sentence stem and explanation of function of evidence:	Sentence stem and explanation of function of evidence:	Sentence stem and explanation of function of evidence:

***Ideas in Literature*, 1e**
Unit 5, p. 663

In the following chart, record some notes to help you communicate the context of your argument, along with introductory details about the narrative situation, extended metaphor, or pattern of imagery. This introductory material will funnel your ideas to your thesis statement. Next, record details to help you explain the relevance of your unifying idea and insight in your concluding statements.

Establishing Context and Explaining Relevance	
Idea and Insight	**Context for Introduction**
	Significance of Idea in Conclusion

***Ideas in Literature*, 1e**
Unit 5, p. 664

After you have completed revising and editing your own argument, review another student's literary argument and provide helpful feedback.

Revising and Editing an Analysis of Imagery/Extended Metaphor		
Revising and Editing Checklist	**Unit 5 Focus Skills**	**Comment on the Effectiveness and/or Make a Suggestion**
Does the writer include the narrative situation, title, and author of the literary text in the first paragraph? Does the brief summary of context and the reference to imagery/extended metaphor lead to the idea?	Introductions for analysis of imagery/extended metaphor	
Does the thesis statement convey an interpretation? Does the interpretation connect to an idea and an insight?	Defensible thesis	
Does the writer provide a logical sequence of reasons to support the idea and insight in the thesis? Are these reasons linked to the claim with transitions?	Line of reasoning: Unity	

Does the writer provide relevant and sufficient evidence to support the interpretation in the thesis? Is the evidence linked to the topic sentences with transitions?	Relevant and sufficient evidence	
Does the writer explain how the evidence supports a reason and connects to the interpretation in the thesis? Does the commentary connect to the unifying idea? Does the writer include transitional elements to create coherence?	Commentary: Unity and coherence	
Does the writer explain significance within a broader context, discuss alternative interpretations, or use relevant analogies?	Relevance	
Does the writer demonstrate control over the conventions of writing?	Conventions	

UNIT 6

Analyzing Representations

***Ideas in Literature*, 1e**
Unit 6, p. 686

As you read Hurston's short story "Spunk," identify characters who contrast with the protagonist. Record details from the text that characterize them. Then explain the significance of these contrasts.

Analyzing Contrasting Characters		
Protagonist: Contrasting characters:		
Attributes of Protagonist	**Attributes of Contrasting Character(s)**	**Significance (What this reveals about the protagonist)**

***Ideas in Literature*, 1e**
Unit 6, p. 695

As you read the chapter "Richie" from Jesmyn Ward's *Sing, Unburied, Sing*, record the details of the plot that occur at the beginning, middle, and end of this chapter. Then identify the nonlinear narrative technique being used and explain what insight the technique offers into Ward's idea in this chapter.

Analyzing Nonlinear Plots		
Moments and Details from the Plot	**Narrative Technique**	**Significance in Relation to the Idea**
Beginning:		
Middle:		
End:		

***Ideas in Literature*, 1e**
Unit 6, p. 705

As you read the excerpt from *The Sympathizer*, note the choices the narrator makes (e.g., what he does, what he says). Consider why the narrator makes these choices and then explain the effect of those choices, especially how they contribute to his reliability.

Analyzing Narrator Reliability		
Narrator's Actions or Choices	**Narrator's Motivation**	**Effect on the Narrative**

***Ideas in Literature*, 1e**
Unit 6, p. 713

As you read Chapter 1 of *A Prayer for Owen Meany*, make note of potential symbols in the text. Describe their symbolic meaning and explain how they contribute to a unifying idea.

Analyzing the Function of Symbols		
Unifying idea:		
Colors, Numbers, Objects, Characters, Animals, Clothing, Places, Seasons, Holidays, Time, Weather	**Symbolic Association**	**Connection to the Idea**

***Ideas in Literature*, 1e**
Unit 6, p. 896

Review the text that you are analyzing for your literary argument. Record your unifying idea, as well as the topic and focus of your analysis. Then, use the graphic organizer to identify details and their significance for different moments in the work. (You may need to delete or add rows).

Analyzing a Symbol		
Unifying idea:		
Topic and focus of analysis:		
Symbol	**Details from the Text**	**Insights and Connections to the Unifying Idea**

***Ideas in Literature*, 1e**
Unit 6, p. 898

Complete the following chart. In the left column, record the title, author, and aspect of the symbol that you will explore in your analysis. Next, record the unifying idea and insight that will convey your interpretation in your claim.

Developing a Thesis Statement for Analysis of Symbol		
Topic	**Claim**	
Title, Author, and Focus (aspect of symbol)	**Unifying Idea +**	**Insight**

Ideas in Literature, **1e**
Unit 6, p. 900

Review your thesis statement, which may or may not preview the line of reasoning. Record the topic sentences to represent your line of reasoning and place them in a logical order. As you do this, consider the potential evidence from the text that helped you arrive at your line of reasoning. That textual evidence will support these reasons.

Developing a Line of Reasoning		
Defensible Thesis Statement with Claim (idea + insight):		
Topic Sentence 1 (Identify the first aspect of the symbol related to the unifying idea):	**Topic Sentence 2** (Identify the second aspect of the symbol related to the unifying idea):	**Topic Sentence 3** (Identify the third aspect of the symbol related to the unifying idea):

***Ideas in Literature*, 1e**
Unit 6, p. 901

Write your thesis statement and develop a logical line of reasoning to support your interpretation. Carefully organize your body paragraphs and arrange the evidence within them. Next, draft two or more body paragraphs that include evidence from the text to support each reason. Include transitions to link your reasons and evidence to your claim.

Incorporating Relevant and Sufficient Evidence		
Defensible Thesis Statement with Claim (idea + insight):		
Topic Sentence 1 (Identify the first aspect of the symbol related to the unifying idea):	**Topic Sentence 2** (Identify the second aspect of the symbol related to the unifying idea):	**Topic Sentence 3** (Identify the third aspect of the symbol related to the unifying idea):
Textual Details (Relevant and sufficient evidence):	**Textual Details** (Relevant and sufficient evidence):	**Textual Details** (Relevant and sufficient evidence):

Ideas in Literature, **1e**
Unit 6, p. 906

Build on your emerging literary argument by adding commentary to your relevant and sufficient evidence. As you plan your explanation, carefully consider when you may need to show balance or imbalance within your commentary. Additionally, keep the focus on your unifying idea so that you may carry this idea throughout your argument in a unified way.

<table>
<tr><th colspan="3">Using Coordination and Subordination to Establish Relationships within the Argument</th></tr>
<tr><td colspan="3">Defensible Thesis Statement with Claim (idea + insight):</td></tr>
<tr><td colspan="3"></td></tr>
<tr><td>Topic Sentence 1
(Identify the first aspect of the symbol related to the unifying idea):</td><td>Topic Sentence 2
(Identify the second aspect of the symbol related to the unifying idea):</td><td>Topic Sentence 3
(Identify the third aspect of the symbol related to the unifying idea):</td></tr>
<tr><td></td><td></td><td></td></tr>
<tr><td>Textual Details
(Relevant and sufficient evidence):</td><td>Textual Details
(Relevant and sufficient evidence):</td><td>Textual Details
(Relevant and sufficient evidence):</td></tr>
<tr><td>Signal phrase and evidence 1:

Signal phrase and evidence 2:</td><td>Signal phrase and evidence 1:

Signal phrase and evidence 2:</td><td>Signal phrase and evidence 1:

Signal phrase and evidence 2:</td></tr>
</table>

Commentary (Link evidence to reason and idea):	**Commentary** (Link evidence to reason and idea):	**Commentary** (Link evidence to reason and idea):
Sentence stem and explanation of function of evidence:	Sentence stem and explanation of function of evidence:	Sentence stem and explanation of function of evidence:

Ideas in Literature, 1e
Unit 6, p. 907

In the following chart, record some notes to help you communicate the context of your argument, the introductory details about the symbol, and the introductory material that will funnel your ideas to your thesis statement. Next, record ideas to help you explain the relevance of your idea and insight in your concluding statements.

Establishing Context and Explaining Relevance	
Idea and Insight	**Context for Introduction**
	Significance of Idea in Conclusion

***Ideas in Literature*, 1e**
Unit 6, p. 908

After you have completed revising and editing your own argument, review another student's literary argument and provide helpful feedback.

Revising and Editing an Analysis of Symbol		
Revising and Editing Checklist	**Unit 6 Focus Skills**	**Comment on the Effectiveness and/or Make a Suggestion**
Does the writer include the narrative situation and perspective, title, and author of the literary text in the first paragraph? Does the brief summary of context and reference to the symbol lead to the idea?	Introductions for analysis of symbol	
Does the thesis statement convey an interpretation? Does the interpretation connect to an idea and an insight?	Defensible thesis	
Does the writer provide a logical sequence of reasons to support the idea and insight in the thesis? Are these reasons linked to the claim with transitions?	Line of reasoning: Unity	

Does the writer provide relevant and sufficient evidence to support the interpretation in the thesis? Is the evidence linked to the topic sentences with transitions?	Relevant and sufficient evidence: Coherence	
Does the writer explain how the evidence supports a reason and connects to the interpretation in the thesis? Does the commentary connect to the unifying idea?	Commentary: Unity and coherence	
Does the writer explain the argument's significance within a broader context?	Relevance	
Does the writer employ strategic syntax to represent equality or inequality of ideas?	Coordination and subordination	
Does the writer demonstrate control over the conventions of writing?	Conventions	

UNIT 7

Analyzing Associations

Ideas in Literature, **1e**
Unit 7, p. 935

As you read "The Demon Lover," consider how details revealed through the story's structure develop a conflict that builds toward a climactic moment resulting in an epiphany for the protagonist. Use the graphic organizer to record details from the text that reveal the character. Explain how the textual details contribute to epiphany.

Analyzing Character Epiphany		
Beginning Textual details that indicate values associated with the protagonist	**Middle** Textual details that indicate the protagonist's choices at the climactic moment	**End** Textual details that illustrate the protagonist's epiphany
Details and effect:	Details and effect:	Details and effect:

***Ideas in Literature*, 1e**
Unit 7, p. 950

As you read Adichie's "Cell One," record details of the contrasting settings. Note the values associated with (or represented by) the details of each setting. Then, consider how the contrast between those settings contributes to an interpretation of a single idea.

Analyzing Changing or Contrasting Settings	
Setting 1:	Setting 2:
Details from the text related to Setting 1:	Details from the text related to Setting 2:
Values associated with Setting 1:	Values associated with Setting 2:
How the contrast of settings or change in setting contributes to a single idea:	

***Ideas in Literature*, 1e**
Unit 7, p. 968

As you read "The Hack Driver," notice how Sinclair Lewis uses a narrator to manipulate the narrative. Record textual details and examples that show specific literary techniques. Then explain how these techniques reveal a single idea or insight that contributes to an interpretation of the text.

Analyzing Narrative Pacing		
Literary Techniques and Elements	**Details from the Text**	**Literary Effect**
Plot Sequence Narrative hook Flashback Antecedent action Foreshadowing Deus ex machina Parallel action Juxtaposition In medias res		
Point of View Dialogue Stream of consciousness Narration Aside Frame story		

Description Details Adjectives Adverbs Verbs		
Syntax Short sentences Long sentences Punctuation		

As you read "The Minister's Black Veil: A Parable," identify the point of view. Then record details from the story that contribute to the narrative reliability. Finally, explain how these details, along with your understanding of the narrator, contribute to your interpretation of the story.

<table>
<tr><th colspan="3">Analyzing Narrative Reliability</th></tr>
<tr><td colspan="3">Who is telling the story?

What is the point of view?</td></tr>
<tr><td>First Person
• What role does this character play in the story?
• What is this character's background?
• What is this character's relationship to other characters?
• Is there any reason not to trust this character?
• What is the character's emotional or psychological state?</td><td>Third Person (Limited)
• How does the narrator's limited knowledge affect the story?
• How does the inclusion or exclusion of details reveal the narrator's bias?
• What is the narrative distance?
• What is the effect of the limited information on the narrative?</td><td>Third Person (Omniscient)
• Does this narrator know everything about all characters?
• How does the inclusion or exclusion of details reveal the narrator's bias?
• What is the narrative distance?
• What is the effect of the comprehensive information on the narrative?</td></tr>
<tr><td>Textual Details</td><td>What the Details Reveal about the Narrator</td><td>Literary Effect</td></tr>
<tr><td></td><td></td><td></td></tr>
<tr><td></td><td></td><td></td></tr>
<tr><td></td><td></td><td></td></tr>
<tr><td></td><td></td><td></td></tr>
</table>

Unit 7, p. 1003

As you read "The Yellow Wallpaper," record the specific details of images that establish a single motif. Then explain how each detail contributes to a specific idea within your interpretation.

Analyzing Motifs	
Pattern or Motif:	
Textual Detail (Specific images that contribute to a pattern or motif):	**Literary Effect** (How the particular detail contributes to the motif, revealing an insight about a single idea):

Ideas in Literature, **1e**
Unit 7, p. 1023

As you read "The Paper Menagerie," record textual details that develop and explain how the origami animals take on figurative meaning by identifying the particular aspects of comparison.

Analyzing Figurative Comparisons		
Subject A—Literal:	**Subject B—Figurative:**	**Idea:**
Description: Aspects, Traits, or Characteristics	**Description: Aspects, Traits, or Characteristics**	**Explanation: Significance of Comparison in Relation to Idea**

***Ideas in Literature*, 1e**
Unit 7, p. 1116

Review the text that you are analyzing for your literary argument. Record your unifying idea, as well as the topic and focus of your analysis. Then, use the graphic organizer to identify settings, record details from the text, and consider the implications or significance of these details as they relate to your unifying idea. (You may need to delete or add rows.)

Analyzing Setting	
Unifying idea:	
Topic and focus of analysis:	
Setting	**Setting** (For contrasting or shifting settings)
Details from the text:	Details from the text:
Insights and connections to the unifying idea:	Insights and connections to the unifying idea:

***Ideas in Literature*, 1e**
Unit 7, p. 1118

Complete the following chart. In the left column, record the title, author, and aspect of the setting that you will explore. Next, record the unifying idea and insight that will convey your interpretation of your claim.

Developing a Thesis Statement for Setting Analysis		
Topic	**Claim**	
Title, Author, and Focus (aspect of setting)	**Unifying Idea +**	**Insight**

***Ideas in Literature*, 1e**
Unit 7, p. 1120

Review your thesis statement, which may or may not preview the line of reasoning. Record the topic sentences to represent your line of reasoning and place them in a logical order. As you do this, consider the potential evidence from the text that helped you arrive at your line of reasoning. That textual evidence will serve as support for these reasons.

Developing a Line of Reasoning		
Defensible Thesis Statement with Claim (idea + insight):		
Topic Sentence 1 (Identify the first aspect of the setting related to the unifying idea):	**Topic Sentence 2** (Identify the second aspect of the setting related to the unifying idea):	**Topic Sentence 3** (Identify the third aspect of the setting related to the unifying idea):

***Ideas in Literature*, 1e**
Unit 7, p. 1121

Write your thesis statement and develop a logical line of reasoning to support your interpretation. Carefully organize your body paragraphs and arrange the evidence within them. Next, draft two or more body paragraphs that include evidence from the text to support each reason. Include transitions to link your reasons and evidence to your claim.

Incorporating Relevant and Sufficient Evidence		
Defensible Thesis Statement with Claim (idea + insight):		
Topic Sentence 1 (Identify the first aspect of the setting related to the unifying idea):	**Topic Sentence 2** (Identify the second aspect of the setting related to the unifying idea):	**Topic Sentence 3** (Identify the third aspect of the setting related to the unifying idea):
Textual Details (Relevant and sufficient evidence):	**Textual Details** (Relevant and sufficient evidence):	**Textual Details** (Relevant and sufficient evidence):

***Ideas in Literature*, 1e**
Unit 7, p. 1123

Build on your emerging literary argument by adding commentary to your relevant and sufficient evidence. Continue to incorporate transitions for coherence and craft your sentences to show balance and imbalance of ideas. Additionally, keep the focus on your unifying idea so that you may carry this idea throughout your argument in a unified way.

Explaining the Significance of Setting		
Defensible Thesis Statement with Claim (idea + insight):		
Topic Sentence 1 (Identify the first aspect of the setting related to the unifying idea):	**Topic Sentence 2** (Identify the second aspect of the setting related to the unifying idea):	**Topic Sentence 3** (Identify the third aspect of the setting related to the unifying idea):
Textual Details (Relevant and sufficient evidence):	**Textual Details** (Relevant and sufficient evidence):	**Textual Details** (Relevant and sufficient evidence):

Commentary (Link evidence to reason and idea)	**Commentary** (Link evidence to reason and idea)	**Commentary** (Link evidence to reason and idea)
Sentence stem and explanation of function of evidence:	Sentence stem and explanation of function of evidence:	Sentence stem and explanation of function of evidence:

***Ideas in Literature*, 1e**
Unit 7, p. 1125

In the following chart, record an idea for a hook to begin your argument. Next, record notes to help you communicate the context of your argument, introductory details about the setting, and introductory material that will funnel your ideas to your thesis statement. Then, record ideas to help you explain the relevance of your idea and insight in your concluding statement.

Establishing Context and Explaining Relevance	
Idea and Insight	**Context for Introduction**
	Hook: **Context:**
	Significance of Idea in Conclusion

Ideas in Literature, **1e**
Unit 7, p.1126

After you have completed revising and editing your own argument, review another student's literary argument and provide helpful feedback.

Revising and Editing an Analysis of Setting		
Revising and Editing Checklist	**Unit 7 Focus Skills**	**Comment on the Effectiveness and/or Make a Suggestion**
Does the writer include an engaging hook, the narrative situation, title, and author of the literary text in the first paragraph?	Introductions for setting analysis	
Does the thesis statement convey an interpretation? Does the interpretation connect to an idea and an insight?	Defensible thesis	
Does the writer provide a logical sequence of reasons to support the idea and insight in the thesis? Are these reasons linked to the claim with transitions?	Line of reasoning: Unity	

Does the writer provide relevant and sufficient evidence to support the interpretation in the thesis? Is the evidence linked to the topic sentences with transitions?	Relevant and sufficient evidence: Coherence	
Does the writer explain how the evidence supports a reason and connects to the interpretation in the thesis? Does the commentary connect to the unifying idea?	Commentary: Unity and coherence	
Does the writer explain significance within a broader context?	Relevance	
Does the writer demonstrate control over the conventions of writing?	Conventions	

UNIT 8

Analyzing Incongruities

***Ideas in Literature*, 1e**
Unit 8, p. 1156

As you read "The Joy of Cooking," identify examples of irony or juxtaposition that create incongruities. Then describe the ideas being contrasted through each incongruity. Finally, explain the effect of that incongruity in relation to the work as a whole.

Analyzing Incongruities		
Authors use irony and juxtaposition to establish incongruities in literary texts. **• Irony: Dramatic, Situational, Verbal** **• Juxtaposition: Paradox, Antithesis, Oxymoron**		
Textual Evidence	**Idea Being Emphasized through the Incongruity**	**Type and Effect of Incongruity**

***Ideas in Literature*, 1e**
Unit 8, p. 1161

As you read "Anecdote of the Jar," identify a symbol that is critical for interpreting the poem. Select details and evidence from the poem associated with the symbol. Then, explain the significance of your textual evidence based on both the context of the poem and the poem's unifying idea.

Analyzing a Symbol in Context	
Symbol: Idea:	
Considerations: • How do symbolic objects, actions, events, characters, and settings contribute to a text's complexity and meaning as a whole? • Which symbol in a text do you recognize from other texts? • How is the symbol's meaning(s) in this text similar to or different from its meaning(s) in other texts?	
Textual Details	**Significance Based on Context**

***Ideas in Literature*, 1e**
Unit 8, p. 1169

As you read "The Haunted Oak," identify the multiple points of comparison. Then explain the significance of each aspect of comparison in relation to a unifying idea.

Analyzing Extended Comparisons		
Literal object of comparison: Unifying idea:		
Aspect of Comparison	**Evidence from the Text**	**Significance of the Aspect of Comparison**

***Ideas in Literature*, 1e**
Unit 8, p. 1208

Review the text that you are analyzing for your literary argument. In the graphic organizer, record your unifying idea, as well as the topic and focus of your analysis. Then, record the element of the text structure you will analyze, details from the text, and the implications or significance of these details as they relate to your unifying idea. (You may need to delete or add rows.)

Analyzing Structure and Irony		
Unifying idea:		
Topic and focus of analysis:		
Text Structure	**Details from the Text**	**Insights and Connections to the Unifying Idea**

Ideas in Literature, **1e**
Unit 8, p. 1210

Complete the following chart. In the left column, record the title, author, and aspect of structure that you will explore. Next, record the unifying idea and insight that will convey your interpretation of your claim.

Developing a Thesis Statement for Analysis of Structure and Irony		
Topic	**Claim**	
Title, Author, and Focus (aspect of structure)	**Unifying Idea +**	**Insight**

***Ideas in Literature*, 1e**
Unit 8, p. 1212

Review your thesis statement, which may or may not preview the line of reasoning. Record the topic sentences to represent your line of reasoning and place them in a logical order. As you do this, consider the potential evidence from the text that helped you arrive at your line of reasoning. That textual evidence will serve as support for these reasons.

Developing a Line of Reasoning		
Defensible Thesis Statement with Claim (idea + insight):		
Topic Sentence 1 (Identify the first aspect of structure related to the unifying idea):	**Topic Sentence 2** (Identify the second aspect of structure related to the unifying idea):	**Topic Sentence 3** (Identify the third aspect of structure related to the unifying idea):

***Ideas in Literature*, 1e**
Unit 8, p. 1213

Write your thesis statement and develop a logical line of reasoning to support your interpretation. Carefully organize your body paragraphs and arrange the evidence within them. Next, draft two or more body paragraphs that include evidence from the text to support each reason. Include transitions to link your reasons and evidence to your claim.

Incorporating Relevant and Sufficient Evidence		
Defensible Thesis Statement with Claim (idea + insight):		
Topic Sentence 1 (Identify the first aspect of structure related to the unifying idea):	**Topic Sentence 2** (Identify the second aspect of structure related to the unifying idea):	**Topic Sentence 3** (Identify the third aspect of structure related to the unifying idea):
Textual Details (Relevant and sufficient evidence):	**Textual Details** (Relevant and sufficient evidence):	**Textual Details** (Relevant and sufficient evidence):

***Ideas in Literature*, 1e**
Unit 8, p. 1215

Build on your emerging literary argument by adding commentary to your relevant and sufficient evidence. Continue to incorporate transitions for coherence and craft your sentences to show balance and imbalance of ideas. Additionally, keep the focus on your unifying idea so that you may sustain it throughout your argument in a unified way.

Explaining the Effect of Structural Choices		
Defensible Thesis Statement with Claim (idea + insight):		
Topic Sentence 1 (Identify the first aspect of structure related to the unifying idea):	**Topic Sentence 2** (Identify the second aspect of structure related to the unifying idea):	**Topic Sentence 3** (Identify the third aspect of structure related to the unifying idea):
Textual Details (Relevant and sufficient evidence):	**Textual Details** (Relevant and sufficient evidence):	**Textual Details** (Relevant and sufficient evidence):

Commentary (Link evidence to reason and idea)	**Commentary** (Link evidence to reason and idea)	**Commentary** (Link evidence to reason and idea)
Sentence stem and explanation of function of evidence:	Sentence stem and explanation of function of evidence:	Sentence stem and explanation of function of evidence:

***Ideas in Literature*, 1e**
Unit 8, p. 1216

In the following chart, record some notes to help you communicate the context of your argument, introductory details about the author's structural choices, and introductory material that will funnel your ideas to your thesis statement. Next, record ideas for your conclusion. Remember that it should explain the relevance of your idea and insight within a broader context.

<table>
<tr><th colspan="2">Establishing Context and Explaining Relevance</th></tr>
<tr><th>Idea and Insight</th><th>Context for Introduction</th></tr>
<tr><td rowspan="3"></td><td>Hook:

Context:</td></tr>
<tr><td>Significance of Idea in Conclusion</td></tr>
<tr><td>Broader Context for Conclusion:</td></tr>
</table>

***Ideas in Literature*, 1e**
Unit 8, p.1217

After you have completed revising and editing your own argument, review another student's literary argument and provide helpful feedback.

Revising and Editing an Analysis of Structure and Irony		
Revising and Editing Checklist	**Unit 8 Focus Skills**	**Comment on the Effectiveness and/or Make a Suggestion**
Does the writer include an engaging hook, the narrative situation, title, and author of the literary text in the first paragraph?	Introductions for analysis of structure and irony	
Does the thesis statement convey an interpretation? Does the interpretation connect to an idea and an insight?	Defensible thesis	
Does the writer provide a logical sequence of reasons to support the idea and insight in the thesis? Are these reasons linked to the claim with transitions?	Line of reasoning: Unity	

Does the writer provide relevant and sufficient evidence to support the interpretation in the thesis? Is the evidence linked to the topic sentences with transitions?	Relevant and sufficient evidence: Coherence	
Does the writer explain how the evidence supports a reason and connects to the interpretation in the thesis? Does the commentary connect to the unifying idea?	Commentary: Unity and Coherence	
Does the writer explain significance within a broader context?	Relevance and conclusion	
Does the writer demonstrate control over the conventions of writing?	Conventions	

UNIT 9

Analyzing Complexities

***Ideas in Literature*, 1e**
Unit 9, p. 1244

As you read the excerpt from *Geek Love*, identify and describe the characters presented. Then, explain their function within the narrative in relation to a thematic idea.

Analyzing Minor Characters		
Minor characters may function within a plot in a number of ways, such as the following: • Provide comic relief • Provide details about other characters • Serve as a foil to major characters • Set a tone or mood for a scene • Provide insight into the historical or cultural setting and related values		
Minor Characters	**Description**	**Function in Relation to Thematic Idea**

***Ideas in Literature*, 1e**
Unit 9, p. 1252

As you read Chapter 10 of *Invisible Man*, identify significant moments in the excerpt's narrative arc. For each moment, find a relevant and meaningful quote. Then, describe how the moment fits into the narrative arc. Finally, explain the significance of the moment by considering how it contributes to the dramatic situation and reveals a thematic idea.

Analyzing Significant Moments of Plot		
Considerations • Which event in a plot has a significant relationship to a character, conflict, another event, or thematic idea? What is the relationship? • How does an event or related set of events cause, develop, or resolve a conflict? • How can an event or related set of events represent competing value systems? • How does the resolution or continuation of a conflict affect a character, plot, narrator, or speaker? • How does an event or related set of events contribute to meaning in the whole work? • How does a conflict contribute to meaning in the whole work? • How does the resolution or continuation of a conflict affect a reader's experience with the text?		
Moment and Important Textual Quote:	**Component of the Plot or Excerpt and Its Function in Relation to Other Moments:**	**Significance in Relation to the Thematic Idea:**

***Ideas in Literature*, 1e**
Unit 9, p. 1273

As you read the excerpt from *All the Light We Cannot See*, identify the multiple narrators. Describe each of their perspectives, and then explain how each contributes to an interpretation that reveals a thematic idea.

Analyzing Narrative Complexities		
Considerations • How does a narrator's or speaker's inclusion or exclusion of particular details affect their reliability? • To what degree is the first-person narrator or speaker aware of their own biases? • What is the relationship between a narrator's or speaker's reliability and a reader's understanding of a character's motivations? • How might a change in tone toward a particular subject over the course of a text indicate a narrator's or speaker's change? • How do the diction, imagery, details, and syntax in a text support multiple tones?		
Narrator and Relevant Quotes:	**Perspective and What It Reveals about Characters or Plot:**	**Significance of Perspective in Relation to a Thematic Idea:**

***Ideas in Literature*, 1e**
Unit 9, p. 1404

Review the text that you are analyzing and your notes from your secondary research sources. Using the graphic organizer, record your unifying idea, as well as the topic and focus of your analysis. Then, identify your sources and record relevant details from the text, as well as the significance of these details to your unifying idea. (You may need to delete or add rows.)

Writing a Source-Based Literary Argument		
Unifying idea: Topic and focus of analysis:		
Literary Text (primary source)	**Relevant Details**	**Insights and Connections to the Unifying Idea**
Secondary Sources	**Relevant Information from the Source**	**Insights and Connections to the Unifying Idea**

***Ideas in Literature*, 1e**
Unit 9, p. 1405

Complete the following chart. In the left column, record the title, author, and literary focus that you will explore. Next, record the unifying idea and insight that will convey your interpretation in your claim.

Developing a Thesis Statement for a Source-Based Literary Argument		
Topic	**Claim**	
Title, Author, and Focus (aspect of literary focus or critical lens)	**Unifying Idea +**	**Insight**

***Ideas in Literature*, 1e**
Unit 9, p. 1407

Review your thesis statement, which may or may not preview the line of reasoning. Record the topic sentences to represent your line of reasoning and place them in a logical order. As you do this, consider the potential evidence from both your literary text and secondary sources that helped you arrive at your line of reasoning. That textual evidence will serve as support for these reasons.

Developing a Line of Reasoning		
Defensible Thesis Statement with Claim (idea + insight):		
Topic Sentence 1 (Identify the first aspect of analysis related to the unifying idea):	**Topic Sentence 2** (Identify the second aspect of analysis related to the unifying idea):	**Topic Sentence 3** (Identify the third aspect of analysis related to the unifying idea):

***Ideas in Literature*, 1e**
Unit 9, p. 1408

Write your thesis statement and develop a logical line of reasoning to support your interpretation. Carefully organize your body paragraphs and arrange evidence from your literary text and from secondary sources within them. Next, draft two or more body paragraphs that include evidence from the text and the secondary sources to support each reason. Include transitions to link your reasons and evidence to your claim, as well as citations for the textual evidence.

Incorporating Relevant and Sufficient Evidence from Primary and Secondary Sources		
Defensible Thesis Statement with Claim (idea + insight):		
Topic Sentence 1 (Identify the first aspect of analysis related to the unifying idea):	**Topic Sentence 2** (Identify the second aspect of analysis related to the unifying idea):	**Topic Sentence 3** (Identify the third aspect of analysis related to the unifying idea):
Supporting Details (Evidence from the literary work that contributes to the focus of analysis):	**Supporting Details** (Evidence from the literary work that contributes to the focus of analysis):	**Supporting Details** (Evidence from the literary work that contributes to the focus of analysis):

Supporting Details (Evidence from secondary sources that contributes to the focus of analysis):	**Supporting Details** (Evidence from secondary sources that contributes to the focus of analysis):	**Supporting Details** (Evidence from secondary sources that contributes to the focus of analysis):

***Ideas in Literature*, 1e**
Unit 9, p. 1411

Build on your emerging literary argument by adding commentary to your relevant and sufficient evidence (for both primary and secondary sources). Continue to incorporate transitions for coherence, and craft your sentences to show the balance or imbalance of ideas. Additionally, keep focusing on your unifying idea so that you may sustain it throughout your argument in a unified way.

Explaining Evidence from Primary and Secondary Sources		
Defensible Thesis Statement with Claim (idea + insight):		
Topic Sentence 1 (Identify the first aspect of analysis related to the unifying idea):	**Topic Sentence 2** (Identify the second aspect of analysis related to the unifying idea):	**Topic Sentence 3** (Identify the third aspect of analysis related to the unifying idea):
Textual Details (Relevant and sufficient evidence from primary source):	**Textual Details** (Relevant and sufficient evidence from primary source):	**Textual Details** (Relevant and sufficient evidence from primary source):

Commentary (Link evidence to reason and idea):	**Commentary** (Link evidence to reason and idea):	**Commentary** (Link evidence to reason and idea):
Sentence stem and explanation of function of evidence:	Sentence stem and explanation of function of evidence:	Sentence stem and explanation of function of evidence:
Textual Details (Relevant and sufficient evidence from secondary source):	**Textual Details** (Relevant and sufficient evidence from secondary source):	**Textual Details** (Relevant and sufficient evidence from secondary source):
Commentary (Link evidence to reason and idea):	**Commentary** (Link evidence to reason and idea):	**Commentary** (Link evidence to reason and idea):
Sentence stem and explanation of function of evidence:	Sentence stem and explanation of function of evidence:	Sentence stem and explanation of function of evidence:

***Ideas in Literature*, 1e**
Unit 9, p. 1413

In the following chart, record some notes to help you communicate the context of your argument, introductory details about the author's structural choices, and introductory material that will funnel your ideas to your thesis statement. Next, record ideas to help you explain the relevance of your idea and insight within a broader context in your conclusion.

<table>
<tr><th colspan="2">Establishing Context and Explaining Relevance</th></tr>
<tr><th>Idea and Insight</th><th>Context for Introduction</th></tr>
<tr><td rowspan="3"></td><td>Hook:

Context:</td></tr>
<tr><td>Significance of Idea in Conclusion</td></tr>
<tr><td>Broader context for conclusion:</td></tr>
</table>

***Ideas in Literature*, 1e**
Unit 9, p.1414

After you have completed revising and editing your own argument, review another student's literary argument and provide helpful feedback.

Revising and Editing a Researched Literary Argument		
Revising and Editing Checklist	**Unit 9 Focus Skills**	**Comment on the Effectiveness and/or Make a Suggestion**
Does the writer include an engaging hook, the focus based on the critical lens, title, and author of the literary text in the first paragraph?	Introductions for literary research	
Does the thesis statement convey an interpretation? Does the interpretation connect to an idea and an insight?	Defensible thesis	
Does the writer provide a logical sequence of reasons to support the idea and insight in the thesis? Are these reasons linked to the claim with transitions?	Line of reasoning	

Does the writer provide relevant and sufficient evidence from the literary text and from secondary sources to support the interpretation in the thesis? Is the evidence linked to the topic sentences with transitions?	Relevant and sufficient evidence: Coherence	
Does the writer explain how the evidence supports a reason and connects to the interpretation in the thesis? Does the commentary connect to the unifying idea?	Commentary: Unity and coherence	
Does the writer explain significance within a broader context, discuss alternative interpretations, or use relevant analogies?	Relevance and conclusion	
Does the writer properly document source information with parenthetical citation and a Works Cited page? Does the writer demonstrate control over the conventions of writing?	Conventions	